This Wound *Is a* World

This Wound *Is a* World

BILLY-RAY BELCOURT

UNIVERSITY OF MINNESOTA PRESS

MINNEAPOLIS • LONDON

Poems featured here have previously been published in *Assaracus: A Journal of Gay Poetry, Decolonization, Red Rising Magazine, mâmawi-âcimowak, SAD Mag, Yellow Medicine Review, The Malahat Review, PRISM International,* and *The New Quarterly.*

Originally published in 2017 by Frontenac House

First University of Minnesota Press edition, 2019

Published by the University of Minnesota Press
111 Third Avenue South, Suite 290
Minneapolis, MN 55401–2520
http://www.upress.umn.edu

Printed in Canada on acid-free paper

The University of Minnesota is an equal-opportunity educator and employer.

25 24 23 22 21   10 9 8 7 6 5 4 3 2

Library of Congress Cataloging-in-Publication Data
Belcourt, Billy-Ray, author.
This wound is a world / Billy-Ray Belcourt.
First University of Minnesota Press edition. | Minneapolis : University of Minnesota Press, 2019. | Includes bibliographical references. |
Identifiers: LCCN 2019006710 (print) | ISBN 978-1-5179-0845-4 (pb)
Classification: LCC PR9199.4.B448 A6 2019 (print) | DDC 811/.6—dc23
LC record available at https://lccn.loc.gov/2019006710

When I go extemporaneously, I lose myself

—José Esteban Muñoz

CONTENTS

PREFACE

I think we have—and can have—a right to be free
—Michel Foucault

Poetry is creaturely. It resists categorical capture. It is a shape-shifting, defiant force in the world. Indeed, it runs counter to the world. The aphorism from Michel Foucault leads me to a description of the poem as an entity that insists on "a right to be free." It is an entity because our skin becomes its and its skin becomes ours. In this way, it bears a theory of nonsingularity—the lyric "I" opens up on itself as well as particularizes; the poem brings us into our bodies and thus readies us for the touch and affection of others. I read and write poetry because it is a time and place to practice radical empathy. Poetry reminds us that there are worlds everywhere, in a gradation of states of flux, many of which are hanging in the balance. If a poem could speak, it might chant: *if freedom has not yet come, let us sing it home!*

This is what I hope my poems have done as they have made their way across Canada and outside it, across its at once rupturing and rupturable border. *This Wound Is a World* marked my curiosity about the poem as a unit of study, where study is construed by Fred Moten as a convergence of suffering, dancing, and walking together.[1] At their most curious and energetic, the poems in this book seek to marshal experience, felt knowledge, and feeling in the service of a kind of anticolonial and/or queer theorizing. Consciously and subconsciously, I endeavored to square up against the long history of racism and homophobia in Canada to render forms of indigeneity and queerness that were "recurrent, eddying, *troublant*,"[2] that in their restlessness could agitate affectively arrested ideas of what it is to live, to grieve, and to be desirous of freedom from the position of queer indigeneity. That is, I experimented with the poem as a time and place to breach the sound barriers of historical ignorance and single-issue politics to posit a futurity for the queer Indigenous.

Dr. Alex Wilson of the Opaskwayak Cree Nation teaches me and us that queer and trans Indigenous and two-spirit youth are subject to some of the most acute and world-shattering forms of violence in Indigenous communities: "our bodies, genders, and sexualities have been regulated in a continuum of violence."[3] How might we strike a note of caution and accusation about the failure of liberal governance and historical reckoning to address the misery that tailgates the lives of the doubly and triply marginalized? With which words do we spin a message about what's needed to fissure the structures of bad feeling that catastrophize our lives?

Keguro Macharia asks: "What kind of knowledge is freedom-building, freedom-creating, freedom-pursuing, freedom-sustaining? What's the relationship between this knowledge and state-sanctioned knowledge? What will ground this freedom-oriented knowledge?"[4] Having witnessed the antifreedom stance of many in higher education, I have come to install optimism and hope in the poem as a geopolitical coordinate to enact this grounding of "freedom-oriented knowledge." If political talk and social theory haven't managed to make life more livable for all on their own, then perhaps poetry can shore up a decolonial knowledge that queers and indigenizes freedom. This is the affective and aesthetic engine that makes my writing possible. The goal is not just to advocate for our right to be free but to insist on it, to demand it. The poem is the terrain for this unruly and differently ruled insistence.

NOTES

1. See https://www.newyorker.com/culture/persons-of-interest/fred-motens-radical-critique-of-the-present.
2. Eve Kosofsky Sedgwick, quoted in Maggie Nelson, *The Argonauts* (Minneapolis: Graywolf Press, 2015), 29.
3. Alex Wilson, "Our Coming In Stories: Cree Identity, Body Sovereignty, and Gender Self-Determination," *Journal of Global Indigeneity* 1, issue 1 (2015): 1–5.
4. See https://thenewinquiry.com/blog/toward-freedom/.

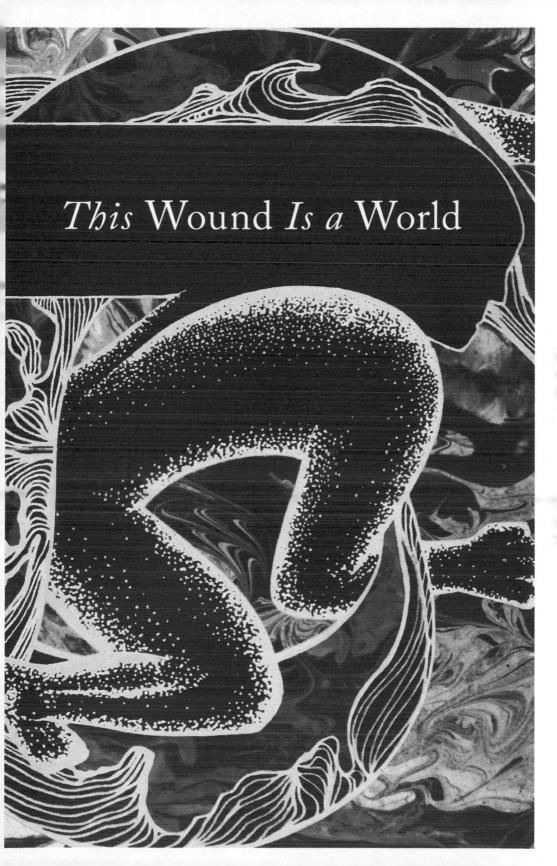

This Wound *Is a* World

love and heartbreak are fuck buddies who sometimes text each other at 10 in the morning. today, love asks: *is this what the living do?* as he tries to shit but can't because he doesn't eat enough fiber or exercise regularly. *it's the little things that'll kill me*, he adds. heartbreak responds, ignoring the first message: *you emptied your body into the floorboards of me. they creak when i Am lonely. if i am a haunted house, then let's make up a theory of negativity that notices the utopian pulse of sad stories like ours. well fuck*, love types out. he deletes it. he sends a selfie with the caption: *how's this for a theory of negativity?* heartbreak laughs. *true*, he quips. love doesn't respond right away. he thinks there is something queer about leaving loose ends untied. love is a native boy from northern alberta who decided almost everything he does is an attempt to repair the brokenness-of-being that is indigeneity. last month, love fucked a security guard in the basement of a parkade at midnight. locking the door behind love, the security guard joked, *don't worry, i'm not going to kill you or anything.* love wonders if it is the possibility of being killed that partly animates his desires. *that's fucked up*, heartbreak tells love when love tells him this story. love hypothesizes that the parkade basement might be a metonym for the world. heartbreak thinks out loud: *how do you know when the world is not that basement anymore?* love answers: *my kookum and mooshum don't use pronouns or proper nouns to address one another. they made their own language. that is how.*

THE CREE WORD FOR A BODY
LIKE MINE IS WEESAGEECHAK

the cree word for a body like mine is *weesageechak*. the old ones know of this kind of shape-shifting: sometimes i sweat and sweat until my bones puddle on the carpet in my living room and i am like the water that comes before new life.

i was born during a falling leaves moon; which is to say that i have always been good at sacrifice. it is believed that women are most powerful during their moontime and because of this do not take part in ceremonies in order to let the body cleanse itself. there are *weesageechak* days when gender is a magic trick i forgot how to perform and my groin floods and floods trying to cleanse itself like the women and i too become toxic for men who have built cages out of broken boys.

maybe if i surrendered myself to grandmother moon she would know what to do with these pickaxe wounds. there is so much i need to tell her about how my rivers and lakes are crowded and narrowing. how i managed to piece together a sweat lodge out of mud and fish and bacteria. she gives me the cree name *weesageechak* and translates it to "sadness is a carcass his tears leave behind."

and the crows and flies who don't care about gender will one day make away with my jet-black finger nails and scraggly armpit hairs. they will lay tobacco at my grave and tell their crow and fly kin that i was once a broad-shouldered trickster who long ago fell from the moon wearing make-up and skinny jeans.

GAY INCANTATIONS

i fall into the opening between subject and object
and call it a condition of possibility.
when i speak only the ceiling listens.
sometimes it moans.
if i have a name,
let it be the sound his lips make.
there is no word in my language for this.
my kookum begins to cry
and then there is a world before me.
grieve is the name i give to myself.
i carve it into the bed frame.
i am make-believe.
this is an archive.
it hurts to be a story.
i am the boundary between reality and fiction.
it is a ghost town.
you dreamt me out of existence.
you are at once a map to nowhere and everywhere.
yesterday was an optical illusion.
i kiss a stranger and give him a middle name.
i call this love.
it lasts for exactly twenty minutes.
i chase after that feeling.
which is to say:
i want to almost not exist.
almost is the closest i can get to the sky.
heaven is a wormhole.
i first found it in another man's armpit.
last night i gave birth to a woman and named her becoming.
she is four cree girls between the ages of 10 and 14 from northern
        saskatchewan.
we are a home movie
i threw out by accident.
all that is left is the signified.
people die that way.

i never dream about myself anymore.
i chose a favorite memory
and named it after every boy
i have broken up with.
grief is easier that way.
i need to cut a hole in the sky
to world inside.
is the earth round,
or is it in the shape of a broken heart?
i drove through a town called freedom
and it looked like an accident
pretending to be a better accident.
there is a city in colorado
called loveland
and it is where alone meets lonely.
i have been there exactly two times.
i saw a lot of indians
and cried for three days afterwards.
i bought a pin that says LOVE
and i wear it on my jean jacket as a cry for help.
i asked all 908 of my facebook friends
to tell me they loved me
and they did
and i believed them.
my cousin's boyfriend punched
a hole in the wall
so i hid inside it
and for a few seconds i thought
maybe this is what heaven looks like.
i ran off the edge of the world
into another world
and there everyone
was at least a little gay.

THERE IS A DIRT ROAD IN ME

there is a dirt road in me.
it takes you to a place like a reserve but not
because there are only cree girls
and no one is falling apart in a bad way.
we are a people
who proliferate
only as potentiality.
do not compare us to the rain
unless you fucking mean it.
why did my love scare you?
was it too dirt road?
what would you have done with a dirt road anyways?

WIHTIKOWAK MEANS "MEN WHO CAN'T SURVIVE LOVE"

1. setting: it is 2013 in a small-town made up of oil dreams and soured masculinity and a thin white man reports a *wihtikow* sighting.

2. legend has it that *wihtikowak* were once cree men whose sins betrayed their bodies until they thickened and thickened and turned into giants the size of spruce trees. these were men who were never holy only selfish enough to want to drown in another man's thighs. in the old days, this kind of closeness was so mystical and sinister it was called cannibalism.

3. if you must know more, know that the thin white man blindfolded himself and fucked the *wihtikow*. that he put his mouth to its ear and whispered, *i will learn to love a monster. wihtikowak* means "men who can't survive love," so each time the thin white man kissed his *wihtikow* it would ache and groan and flinch but still ask for more until it stopped breathing and melted into the mattress. i think it felt something like freedom.

THE REZ SISTERS II

after tomson highway

cast:

girl of surplus. girl who is made from fragments. she who can only be spoken of by way of synecdoche. she whose name cannot be enunciated only mouthed.

mother of that which cannot be mothered. mother who wants nothing and everything at the same time. she who gave birth to herself three times: 1. the miscarriage. 2. the shrunken world. 3. the aftermath.

sister of forest fire. sister who dwells in the wreckage. she who forages for the right things in the wrong places. nothing is utopia and so she prays to a god for a back that can bend like a tree splitting open to make room for the heat.

aunt of the sovereignty of dust. aunt of that which cannot be negated entirely. she who is magic because she goes missing and comes back. she who walks upside down on the ceiling of the world and does not fall.

kookum of love in spite of it all. kookum who made a man out of a memory. she who is a country unto herself.

father of ash. father of a past without a mouth. he who ate too much of the sunset.

SIX THESES ON WHY NATIVE PEOPLE DIE

1. indigeneity exceeds and is exceeded by gender.

2. he couldn't make language out of the gravel-like noise stuck in his throat.

3. once freed from the bottom of his stomach, desire went on a killing spree.

4. she made a casket out of his guilt.

5. we were a sad story and i fell in love with the idea of it.

6. she watched a western and thought the world looked better in black and white.

SACRED

a native man looks me in the eyes as he refuses to hold my hand during
a round dance. his pupils are like bullets and i wonder what kind of pain
he's been through to not want me in this world with him any longer.
i wince a little because the earth hasn't held all of me for quite some time
now and i am lonely in a way that doesn't hurt anymore.

you see, a round dance is a ceremony for both grief and love and each
body joined by the flesh is encircled by the spirits of ancestors who've
already left this world. i ask myself: how many of them gave up on desire
because they loved their kookums more than they loved themselves?

i dance with my arm hanging by my side like an appendage my body
doesn't want anymore. the gap between him and me keeps getting bigger
so i fill it with the memories of native boys who couldn't be warriors
because their bodies were too fragile to carry all of that anger. the ones
who loved in that reckless kind of way. you know, when you surrender
your body to him.

and i think about the time an elder told me to be a man and to decolonize
in the same breath. there are days when i want to wear nail polish more
than i want to protest. but then i remember that i wasn't meant to live life
here and i paint my nails because 1) it looks cute and 2) it is a protest. and
even though i know i am too queer to be sacred anymore, i dance that
broken circle dance because i am still waiting for hands that want to hold
mine too.

in the 1990s,
a man raped a little girl
and the reserve caught fire.
it never stopped burning.
i mouthed the word *justice*
and then forgot how to speak.
if these walls could talk
they would sing country songs
about an entire generation of men who learned how to love on grindr.
    what did you expect, my love?
alternate ending:
i give my body to men
i don't find attractive
and it doesn't fuck me up.
12:03 am: why is it that love makes you feel lonely?
if the earth
could end it all right now
i think it would.
what i know:
    colten boushie
    a ceremonial fire keeper
    was shot while sitting in the backseat of a car with a flat tire;
    and
    it took an ocean to break us.

WE WERE NEVER MEANT TO BREAK LIKE THIS

1. follow me out the backdoor of the world.

2. how do you tell someone that they are helping you stay tuned into life?

3. what does it mean that her first breath was also her last?

4. i am so sad that i burrow into the absence of every boy who has held me.

5. i kiss him knowing that when i wake up i will be in a body differently.

6. the future is already over, but that doesn't mean we don't have anywhere else to go.

I AM HOPING TO HELP THIS CITY
HEAL FROM ITS TRAUMA

"i am hoping to help this city heal from its trauma."

i sleep with a man who looks like he is dying. his eyes are caves, darkened skin disappears them. with each movement, his body wrings and protests. i think sex is the only thing that can stop the hurt for a little while. perhaps this is what being medicine feels like.

"i am hoping to help this city heal from its trauma."

he messages me at 3 am and i respond because my phone vibrates and wakes me up. he tells me he is horny, that his roommate is working night shift, and that he wants someone to piss into his mouth tonight. he sends me a picture of his dick and confesses that he's had a bit of ecstasy but that it doesn't affect him much anyways. i want to know what it's like for my body to end in someone else so i travel twenty minutes to his apartment and stay for three hours. when i leave he admits that he's closeted, but that he would like to see me soon to open himself up to desire again.

"i am hoping to help this city heal from its trauma."

when we fuck, we meet in his RV in the dark. i never see his entire face, but i think there's something romantic about the way we disappear into each other. he's twenty years older than i am and softly calls me a bitch over and over again when he cums. i don't ask why he's whispering and i think someone is waiting inside the house for him and maybe they always do. maybe he learnt love like disappearing into things that aren't good for him.

"i am hoping to help this city heal from its trauma."

he asks me how many men i've slept with and i lie and say seven. he
thinks that's too many because he's thirty and has only been with three
men and one woman, his ex-wife. he asks me to spend the night and i
do because sometimes i just need to be next to a body like his. later, he
breaks up with me because i reminded him of everything he's ever had
stolen from him. being with me, he says, was like living inside a cemetery.

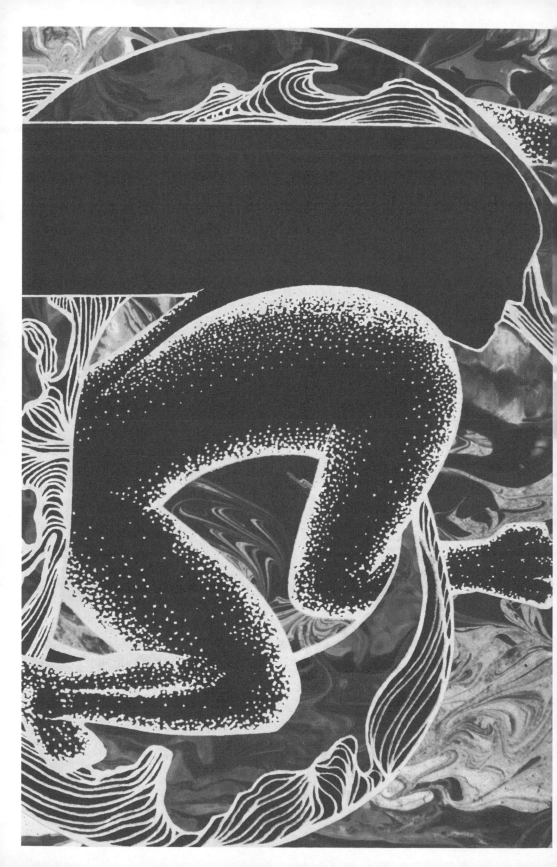

HEARTBREAK IS A WHITE KID

heartbreak is a white kid from south edmonton
who lives inside the what-had-been.
the what-had-been is an atmosphere,
a sensation against which all others are calculated.
it is a performance of embodiment,
or should i say disembodiment?
heartbreak is a body that is not bodied.
he is everything that will have happened to him:
he is his mother first
and then his sister, both dead.
heartbreak is an alias.
it is not a name but an enactment of grief
whereby one ropes strangers by the tongue into a collective wounding.
heartbreak lives in the underbelly of a system
meant to world around his body.
heartbreak is sonic:
it is the sound one makes when one becomes
those who refuse to be put to rest.
heartbreak is the first man with whom i fell in love.
heartbreak is the sound
we made when we bodied one another with things like cum and tears
        and saliva.
that our eyes stopped
believing in what was in front of us
was the closest we got to killing ourselves.

i keep listening to a song by tom odell called *grow old with me*. i am hung up on the enormity of that kind of project, of asking someone to architect a livable world with you. what a blessing and a curse!

i hooked up with a man who insisted he was 42, but i suspect he was older given the soft and reckless way he met my body with his. it was 9 pm and we were making small talk and he told me a story about how a relationship of his had started and ended at the same ski resort in france. recently, he returned to that resort, and was caught unawares by a wave of memories about his ex-boyfriend. today, he lives alone in a houseboat, unwilling to be beside himself with desire. how could he have expected anything but what christina sharpe calls "the past that is not past" to haunt him? maybe that is why he wanted to sleep with me last night. maybe that is why i invited him over in the first place. i should have said: *i don't have it in me to transform you.*

if i have a body, let it be a book of sad poems. i mean it. indigeneity troubles the idea of "having" a body, so if i am somehow, miraculously, bodied then my skin is a collage of meditations on love and shattered selves.

ok yes, i have been reading a bit of psychoanalysis lately. forgive me. i am desperate. desperate to figure out how someone like me is still here.

if i know anything, it is that "here" is a trick of the light, that it is a way of schematizing time and space that is not the only one available to some of us. maybe i am not here in the objectivist sense. maybe i am here in the way that a memory is here. now, ain't that fucking sad and beautiful?

GRIEF AFTER GRIEF AFTER GRIEF AFTER GRIEF

1. my body is a stray bullet. i was made from crossfire. love was her last
   resort. his mouth, a revolver. i come from four hundred no man's lands.

2. "smell my armpit again / i miss it when you do that."

3. his moaning is an honor song i want to world to.

4. one of the conditions of native life today is survivor's guilt.

5. it is july 2016 and the creator opens up the sky to attend a
   #blacklivesmatter protest. there, she bumps into *weesageechak* and
   warns him that if policemen don't stop killing black men she will
   flood america and it will become a lost country only grieving mothers
   will know how to find. this, she says, is how the world will end and
   be rebuilt this time.

6. haunting is a gender. gender is another word for horror story.

7. "i can hear him screaming for me, and i can hear him saying, 'stop,
   honey help me.'"

8. i am trying to figure out how to be in the world without wanting it.
   this, perhaps, is what it means to be native.

the creator is trans
and the earth is a psychology experiment
to determine how quickly
we mistake a body for anything
but a crime scene
the product of older crime scenes.
there is a heaven
and it is a place called gay.
gay as in let's hold up a world together.
gay as in happy to make something out of nothing
and call it love or anything
that resembles a time
in which you don't have to be those shitty versions of yourself
to become who you are now.
one day i will open up my body
to free all of the people i've caged inside me.
i want to visit every tim hortons in northern alberta
so that homophobes can tell me sad things like
i love you
your hair looks nice
you have nice cheekbones
until someone kills me
and then the creator will write my eulogy
with phrases like
freedom is the length of a good rim job
and *the most relatable thing about him*
was how often he cried watching wedding videos on youtube.
homonationalism, amirite?
my grandma thought there was a portal
to the other side in her basement
but it was all of the women she had ever met
praying in a circle
that she would give birth to a world
without men
only women
made
from other women's heartbreak.

THE BACK ALLEY OF THE WORLD

make my mouth into a jar
spit inside me
throw me into the air
leave me there
pretend that this is love.
whisper: *tonight, we will be children*
tomorrow, the feeling of being in two bodies at once.
pray, if it gives you a tongue
a book for words that fall flat
a book that does not like to be written in.
where do you come from?
i am from the back alley of the world.

he was native too
so i slept with him.
i wanted to taste
a history of violence
caught in the roof of his mouth.
i wanted our saliva to mix
and create new bacterial ecologies:
contagions that could infect
the trauma away.
i wanted to smell his ancestors
in his armpits:
the aroma of their decaying flesh,
how they refuse to wilt into nothingness.
i wanted to touch his brown skin
to create a new kind of friction
capacious enough
for other worlds to emerge
in our colliding.
i wanted our tongues
to sketch a different tomorrow:
one in which we might know how to love better,
again.
i wanted him to fuck me,
so i could finally begin
to heal.

COLONIALISM: A LOVE STORY

1. colonialism broke us, and we're still figuring out how to love and be broken at the same time.

2. the first time he told me i was beautiful, i thought he was lying. i thought beauty was a plot in a story i had been written out of a long time ago.

3. what happens when "i love you, too" becomes a substitute for "i can't," when his hand finds your body and it feels like he's taking pieces of it? perhaps this is what they meant by "love requires sacrifice."

4. sometimes bodies don't always feel like bodies but like wounds.

5. he told me he'd take a needle and stitch our bodies together with the thickest thread.

6. colonialism. definition: turning bodies into cages that no one has the keys for.

7. when i invite him into the abandoned house of me, he tiptoes inside. he notices the way the walls ache to be touched again even though they know time won't let them survive it.

8. we need not pretend that love was to be found in wastelands like these.

GOD'S RIVER

it is september 2009 and health canada sends body bags to god's river
first nation — a community hit hard by swine flu

a body bag
is a gun
is a smallpox blanket
is a treaty
— call it a medicine chest

wait for
an autopsy
they call it H1N1
you call it
the pass system:
bodies like
these can
only leave if
they're on
stretchers
— call it "moving"

someone says:
"it's like sending
body bags
to soldiers in
afghanistan"

remind them
that canada is
four hundred
afghanistans
— call it colonialism

to live in
trenches like these
is to be
civilian casualty
and soldier all at once
– call it a "suicide epidemic"

wonder
how many deaths
it takes for a
country to
call itself
god

think maybe
reserve is
another word
for morgue
is another word
for body bags
– call it home anyways

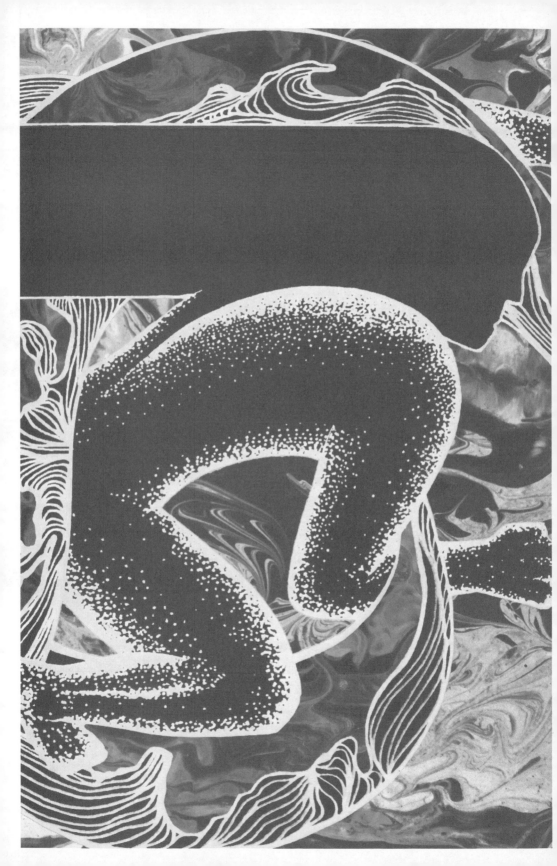

LOVE AND OTHER EXPERIMENTS

1. he told me he was into natives, but he couldn't love the traumas hidden in my breathing.

2. how do you tell a ghost that it's already dead?

3. what happens when wounds start to work like bandages?

4. sometimes love feels like vanishing, like taking apart pieces of yourself and giving them to someone who can't use them.

5. what happens when decolonial love becomes a story you tell yourself after he falls asleep?

6. i tell him: *you breathe us. we are in you. look at the blood on your hands.*

7. queer. definition: knowing your body is both too much and not enough for this world.

8. i asked the earth to hold all of me and it said *i can't. i can't keep making room for everyone much longer.*

9. sometimes not loving is the most radical thing you can do.

OKCUPID

my okcupid username was *nakinisowin*
which in cree means: resistance
means: not white
means: love don't live here
means: ask me what my "ethnicity" is
and say *that's interesting*
when i tell you i'm native

that i am the monster in the closet
your bedtime stories prepared you for
you want a man
whose body doesn't whisper
horror stories
each time you touch him
a man whose nightmares are about dying
because he doesn't already know what that feels like

but then i messaged *mrBoB*
because his skin was brown
like the water that drags itself through my reserve
pleading:
drink me
i need you
i promise
and his profile was a eulogy of sorts
he was still in mourning
refusing to let go of a body
which never belonged to him in the first place

i said: *hey*
to which he responded: *be careful*
i am still healing from the white men who told me they loved me
and my cree is broken like my body is
and i don't know how to tell the difference between love and trauma
but i could try
for you
a native
like me

which is to say that to be native and queer
is to sometimes forget how to love yourself
because no one else wants to
is to bandage the wounds with strangers
you met an hour ago
and count the number of times
they baptize you with words like
beautiful and handsome and sexy
because sex is the only ceremony
you have time for
these days

but this was different
because time stops
and is made anew
when two native boys
find each other's bodies
and write poems about it afterwards
because each kiss was an act of defiance
a kind of nation-building effort
our bodies were protesting
dancing in a circle
to the beat of
a different drum
that was also
a world in and of itself

TOWARDS A THEORY OF DECOLONIZATION

1. forget everything you've learned about love.

2. investment is the social practice whereby one risks losing it all to be a part of something that feels like release. lose everything with me.

3. indian time is a form of time travel. a poetics of lateness.

4. i never liked goodbyes, but some of us aren't here to stay.

5. superstition is a mode of being in the world that keeps ghosts like me in the living room.

6. the afterlife is the after party: a choreography of mangled bodies.

7. i made a poem out of dirt and ate it.

do we have a word to make sense of this kind of loss: a body feeling like it doesn't belong to you anymore? sometimes the act of enduring itself becomes too much to bear and you forget how to go on in a world that didn't want you in the first place. how do you mourn something you can still see in the mirror?

everyone is lonely
but no one knows
what to do about it.
once a week
i curate
obituaries
on my facebook wall
without even trying.
the wind
makes away
with parts of my body but i don't
notice the difference.
my mom
couldn't get enough
of the sight
of broken twigs
and thus
i was born.
i am single
because i haven't dated
anyone who is
broken twig enough.
he's a little bit
country,
i'm a little bit
barbed-wire fence.

a guy like u doesn't belong on grindr lol
1:54 am

> there is no beautiful left
> last week i choked up every time i spoke
> this is the closest i'll get to speaking my language
> 1:55 am

are u lookin for a man with an ocean in him
2:12 am

> once upon a time
> i only fuck men who know i am beautiful for all the wrong reasons
> 2:12 am

> [the past pours itself onto my feet]
> did it hurt when you dropped us from the sky, nikawiy
> 2:20 am

what is the cost of falling into a body like yours
2:25 am

> my safe word is *amen*
> 2:27 am

BOYFRIEND POEMS

1. when he holds my hand in public i think someone might call us faggots. i wish they would.

2. i die each time he tells me he loves me. he taught me how to live forever.

3. femininity is a torch only the bravest men can carry.

4. sometimes our bodies obey in explaining our desires before we do. are you listening?

5. *are you femme? because i'm not interested in that.*

6. there are days when it feels like my body is trying to hurt me, anchoring me in a world in which native means lonely and lonely feels a lot like dying.

7. my body, like the land, was up for grabs.

8. it was the drunk elephant in the room.

GOD MUST BE AN INDIAN

god must be an indian, he said
for so many of you speak like the sky.
maybe i am a figure of speech.
maybe my body is an inside joke that we're all in on.
now is a time for metaphor.
give me a gender,
but only if it is something like a candlelight vigil.
remember: grief is a way of making claim to the world.
my kookum asked: *is there something indian about crying?*
tonight, i will take my former lovers in my arms
and convince them that i am not a graveyard.
in the dark, none of us has names and no one is sacred.
god must be an indian, he said.
this is not a love poem.

SEXUAL HISTORY

1. i tell my dad i want to be a rainbow when i grow up. my body is a jar of my mother's tears that shape-shifts in the sunlight.

2. in eighth grade i date a girl whose parents think i am not manly enough for her. i am relieved to be neither wildfire nor prison cell.

3. i call my kookum to tell her i have a boyfriend and that she will meet him in ten minutes. i piece together a world inside the quiet before her next breath and name it earth.

4. all of the men i date happen to be white. turns out i am good at loving those who broke open the world. i can't decide if this is ironic or heartbreaking.

5. i am one of those hopeless romantics who wants every blow job to be transformative.

6. when i am old i hope the moon spots me one day and is like *wow i remember when he thought getting fucked was like disappearing into someone for a few seconds.*

7. note to self: shouldn't the creator be angry by now? even i know what it's like to watch everything disappear into everything else.

TIME CONTRA TIME

my body is an open casket:
i am made up of dead things
young, old, and ageless.
i kiss every white man
who looks at me
like i am splitting at the seams.
i tell them to call me *yesterday*
to remind them that they are fucking a ghost
and that they did this
and are doing this to me.
when you are a ghost
all time is unlived time.
which is to say
that time uninhabits you.
unlived time is funeral time
is how long it takes to let go of a childhood.
i kiss every native man
who looks at me
like i am splitting at the seams.
i tell them to call me *rendered*
since to rend
is to tear into pieces
is to rip and sever and split
such that one can be rendered again.
since to render
is to cause to be or to become:
an aesthetics of incarnation.

1. we've known for weeks that this wasn't going to work out. but we
    tried anyways, like all indians do.

2. it's ironic, i think: that love and despair can fill out a body together
    and we call it *indian*.

3. i lay on his chest knowing the best and worst thing about him
    is the way his skin protests forgetting.

4. lonely enough to think that things will be different this time,
    she drinks from a sad man's lungs.

5. take this body and do not say you see anything but a pile of
    shattered glass.

6. there are days when being in life feels like consenting to the
    cruelties that hold up the world.

ODE TO NORTHERN ALBERTA

after joshua jennifer espinoza

here, no one is birthed
only pieced together.
i tire myself out
pretending to have a body.
everyone worships feelings
they don't have names for
but no one is talking about it.
love is a burning house we built from scratch.
love keeps us busy while the smoke clears.
history lays itself bare
at the side of the road
but no one is looking.
history screams into the night
but it sounds too much like the wind.
cree girls gather in the bush
and wait for the future.
in the meantime
they fall in love with the trees
and hear everything.
in the 1950s
my not-yet mooshum ran away
from a residential school
in joussard, alberta.
as an adult
he kept coming back
despite knowing
heaven is nowhere near here.

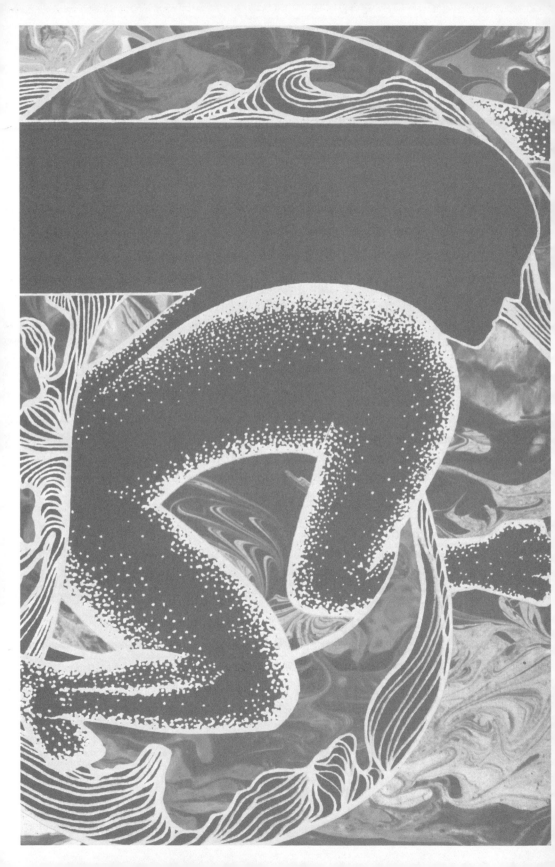

I

you notice the regularity with which others avoid confrontation vis-à-vis racial oppression. this is how they think themselves outside of the world. you don't know what it is like to be in a body without it feeling like a death trap. at your desk you watch a news clip of a truck running over native protestors in reno, nevada. no one dies this time. the west is nothing if not a string of murders incriminated by a series of attempted murders.

II

how does it feel to be an object? you wear your favorite pair of ripped jeans, exposing your brown flesh to the world. this exposure is interpreted as an invitation, compelling a stranger in a centuries-old building to walk up to you, rub your skin, laugh, and walk away. you laugh too, but only because your body needs to escape itself, to identify something of an ontological rupture. this is what it feels like to almost not exist. you keep surviving anyway.

III

you attend a mandatory session on intellectual disagreement where you are encouraged to open yourself up to speech. claudia rankine: "language that feels hurtful is intended to exploit all the ways that you are present." you decide that the history of the colonial world is a history of natives being too present. with each word, you thicken and thicken until you burst. these are moments in which other worlds seem impossible.

you are midway through an article on ideology critique when the author makes a reference to primitives who pray for rain. this, he argues, is an example of an ideological defect whereby patterns of behavior serve ends that are cheaply related to those forces (here, social solidarity). you are troubled by the invocation of primitives as if it were prior to ideology, as if it were an anthropological given. more immediately, you pause because this is the first native you encounter in england. you are both empty signifiers.

V

"oxford university embroiled in race row as students told to be 'vigilant' after black man seen in grounds." christina sharpe insists that anti-blackness is a "total climate," that anti-blackness is "pervasive as climate." it is the weather. in oxford the weather allows university staff to speak of blackness as that which begets "vigilance," as that which is an "unauthorized person," as that which catches some "unaware." those of us who study and live in oxford know that the weather is always grey. but, it is also anti-black.

VI

you are called "wonderfully exotic." a man looks at you, tilts his head, and presses that you are "too mixed" for him to pinpoint any sort of ethnic belonging. this is a world-threatening feeling: to be so other that you barely exist in a place whose imperial conquests sought the destruction of your people. when you tell him you are native he doesn't say anything. he lets the silence do the talking, as if he were lamenting the violence that went into producing someone like you. i can tell he has heard a thing or two about us. "i have never met a native american before," he adds, quieter this time. perhaps speaking in a hushed voice makes you less real. what does one do with the sense of loss that tailgates their body?

VII

your body is a catch-22. how does one survive losing one's bearings without an exit strategy? for philosopher jill stauffer, one can feel resistant to existence when their sense of autonomy disappears from the realm of everyday life. it can also occur when one cannot escape what cornel west called "the normative gaze of the white man." the normative gaze of the white man is the air you breathe. it makes a jail out of your lungs. this is what it is to live an existential limbo.

VIII

you and a friend are going for coffee after a lecture on marxist feminist theory and a white british man nudges you with his shoulder. your friend goes to grab a table, a table that he was also intending to grab. he gets visibly upset and, willfully and passionately, says *i'm just trying to get away from you people*. your friend is stunned and in the meantime he returns to say something else under his breath. at this point, you confront him and tell him that he is out of line even though you know that the world is his to claim. he walks away, but throws more words at you. the violence of *you people* is that it is a classic interpellative call, one that pulls you outside yourself, that seeks to trap you in a flattened form of subjectivity. for him, we were nothing. this is the ebb and flow of everyday life in oxford.

IX

you want to capture the sense of a present that is not quite *the* present, a present that thickens in the underbelly of social reality. you stalk the prefix un-, hoping that it will let you see glitches, that it will unearth a hole in the ground, something of a gateway to a world you are spotting any- and everywhere, a world you are spotting nowhere. you are sad, so at first you believe that an un- can be found in the bodies of men. you begin looking for doors, not enclosures. doors without locks. doors that swing open. soon, you decide that doors are a transference of cacophonous feeling; they are ecological, unseen. leanne simpson: "she is the only doorway to this world." the un- is a woman like your kookum who rips open time.

IF OUR BODIES COULD RUST,
WE WOULD BE FALLING APART

the law mandates that a hate crime only be classified as such if there is ample evidence to show that one's actions were motivated by prejudice toward an individual's nationality, ethnicity, sexuality, gender, etc.

oh, i got one!

some more than others know that all objects can be put to violent use. if our bodies could rust, we would be falling apart.

oh, i got one!

barbara kentner, 34, was hit in the stomach by a trailer hitch thrown at her from a moving car. after throwing the hitch, a blond eighteen-year-old man yelled *oh, i got one*. her sister saw and heard everything. no one should have to watch a world explode like that. no one should have to watch someone become unbodied like that. the cbc reported that the police did not investigate the assault as a hate crime because there "were no comments which made any reference to race or ethnicity."

oh, i got one!

it is basic syntax. *one* is the object and she is at the mercy of the *i*. this is a semiotics of indigeneity that routes us into death worlds. in the mouths of the grim reapers of the world, grammar is excited by violence.

oh, i got one!

what did he see when he made her into a ghost? what is a ghost but the form we take when we are pulled outside of our bodies?

oh, i got one!

there were memories made and they do not disappear with the disappeared. kentner was sent home by doctors so that her loved ones could witness her parting. how can a living room become a church without grief leaving its indelible mark?

oh, i got one!

how do we live at the edge of the world?

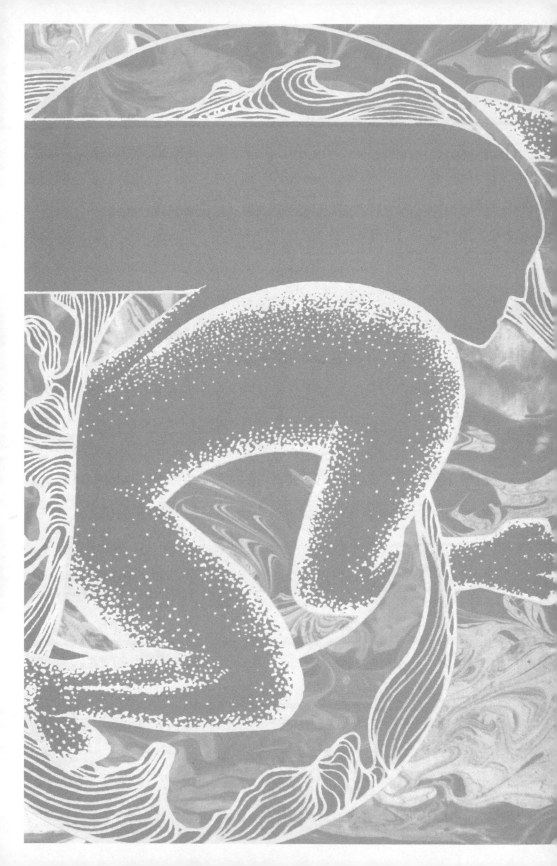

when love looks
into the rubble
of heartbreak
he sees his
kookum
standing there
and he thinks
about how
she made
old worlds
feel livable
again
and about
how those
who died
already
never forget
what it is
to become
and unbecome
a body

WAPEKEKA

in january 2017
two girls, 12, carried out a suicide pact
on the wapekeka first nation.
what is suicide
but the act of opening up
to the sky?
what is suicide
but wanting to live
more than once?
yesterday
a cloud fell onto me
and i never felt more at home.
sometimes i cry
in indian
and it sounds like
i am speaking
in english.
don't open your eyes.
pretend that
everything is a bird
and no one is hungry
for what they can't have.

ODE TO NATIVE MEN

if yesterday never comes,
        if today is today
and no one waits
        with cupped hands
at history's barbed-wire door,
        let us hang our grief up to dry.
yes, there will be wet grass
        at our feet. this is how
we will relearn touch,
        with a river of longing flowing backwards through us.
no, do not think of gravity,
        the earth's brutish appetite.
remember: there is so much september
        before a country begins,
so plant your fists
        in summer's dying days.
now, now you are ready
        to face love's beastly maw
and smile back.

TO SPEAK OF THE DEAD,
I MUST BEGIN WITH THE PHOTON

*The largest mass hanging in Canadian history was at
Battleford, Saskatchewan, in 1885, where eight Indigenous
men were hanged for their participation in the North-West
Rebellion. Indigenous children from the nearby Industrial
School were forced to watch.*

—Aimée Craft

to speak of the dead,
i must begin with the photon:
how it, when caught in a line of sight,
goes on to shatter inside a face.
there are words to describe what this makes of us,
but i won't go there. not today.
not when cumulus clouds
are evaporating at sixty minute intervals.
everything is becoming less of itself everywhere all the time,
and yet the average eyeball is just 24 millimeters wide.
to build the cree word for bloodshed,
you need the modifier *mistahi*, which designates quantity—much,
     a great deal, a lot.
on the other hand, the english word human
originates from *humanus*, a latin word meaning humane, kind, gentle.
of course we have come to know ourselves
by what we are not, much like the modern zoo animal
that, when driven mad by boredom, presses the cage into its mouth.

one need but crane up at the night sky to be reminded of
        our funereal disposition.
how fitting, for example, that we coax the celestially departed
        into the coffins of us!
the plot twist is that we too are like stars:
even after death, the human body emits photons,
        invisible to the naked eye.
think, then, of the hanged men,
who went on to exist, if only for a fraction of a second, as light
inside those war-torn children.
what power is to be won and lost
in the long tradition of Canadian autopsy!

HERMENEUTICS OF THE SOMETIMES/SOMEWHERE

1. the present is a non-world. don't let the flowers lead you
   to a different conclusion.

2. upend cruel nostalgia!

3. there is joy to be made in a utopia without teleology.

4. smudge me with the lights out.

5. i am looking not for water but the tonality of it; to drink in
   the noise of red freedom.

6. the otherworldly is a category of the experience of indigeneity.

7. be against the racialized embargo on care that is canada!

8. the eye of the state is not the eye of providence! perhaps
   there is an underground in which to celebrate our ontological
   fugitivity.

9. the poem: an ontology of ghosts.

10. a theoretics of the doorway is a revolutionary undertaking.

11. remember: loneliness is an emotional performance of a
    world-to-come.

LOVE IS A MOONTIME TEACHING

love is a moontime teaching
is your kookum's crooked smile when you pick up the phone
is another word for body
body is another word for campfire smoke
campfire smoke is the smell he leaves behind in your bed sheets
     after the breakup
the word for hate sex is forest
forest sometimes means hope or lonely (depends on who you ask)
lonely is a movie called *taxi zum klo* about white gay men
who risk tiptoeing through desire's minefields
for ten minutes of something better than living
living is going to bingo to pay the bills
after you quit your job that barely paid the bills
paying the bills is sometimes a metaphor for cancer
cancer is a diagnosis handed down to an 18-year old girl from the rez
the rez is another word for body
the body is a myth
is the only good news the doctor gives you when your cells run amok
amok is the border the skin doesn't remember
how to secure anymore
anymore is the feeling you get when a police officer
pulls you over because he thinks you're driving a stolen vehicle
a stolen vehicle is the nickname you give to love.

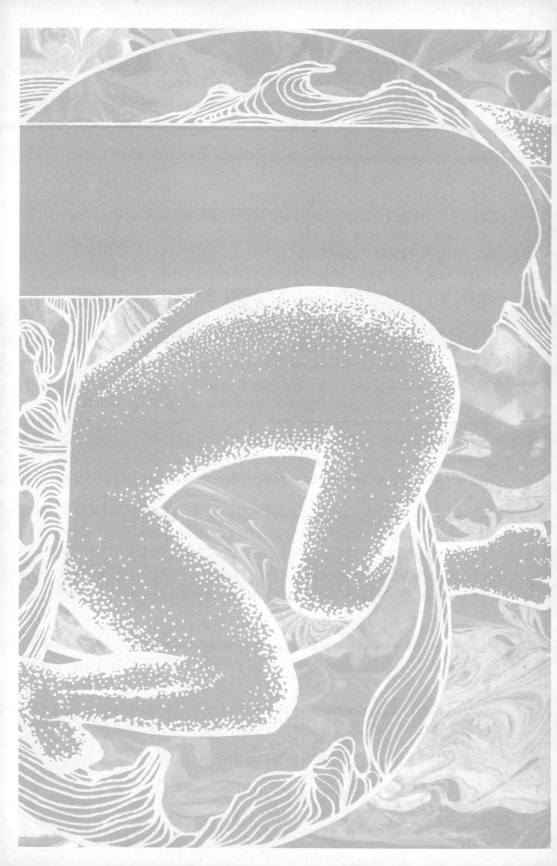

Love, says cultural theorist Laurent Berlant, "always means non-sovereignty,"[1] but only if we think of love as what opens us up to that which feels like it can rupture the ground beneath our feet. Berlant insists that love requires that we violate our own attachments, that we give into instability, that we accept that turbulence is the condition of relationality as such. We might agree, then, that love is a process of becoming unbodied; at its wildest, it works up a poetics of the unbodied.

This Wound Is a World is a book obsessed with the unbodied. It is a book that chases after a scene that can barely be spotted. It is a book that liked to be written only if I stared long enough in the direction of nowhere, which is probably more accurately everywhere. Everywhere, of course, is the space that death carves into everyday life.

It seems difficult to speak of or to ontologize indigeneity without conjuring sadness and death. Take, for example, Angela Davis's speech at the Women's March on Washington on January 21, 2017: "We know that we gather this afternoon on Indigenous land and we follow the lead of the first peoples who *despite massive genocidal violence* have never relinquished the struggle for land, water, culture, their people."[2] I evoke Davis here not to criticize her wording but rather to nod to the way "massive genocidal violence" stalks indigeneity, as if death and indigeneity were co-constitutive categories. I am also not saying that this is always-already bad for us and that we need to tautly commit to positive affect when storying Indigenous life. I think our closeness to sadness and to misery enables a reworking of the codes of bad affect, enabling us to free them from the apoliticized cages of pathology and the private. In her inspiring book *Depression: A Public Feeling*, Ann Cvetkovich argues that bad feeling might actually "be the ground for transformation."

Let's consider a passage from Leanne Simpson's beautiful and world-making collection of stories and songs, *Islands of Decolonial Love*: "i think we fucked, and maybe i should say make love, but maybe not because we didn't actually make love. it was sadder than that. we were sadder than that. but it wasn't bad and it wasn't wrong. it wasn't desperate. i think it was salvation." To be unbodied is the "sadder than that" of love, but it is also love's first condition of possibility. That indigeneity births us into a relation of nonsovereignty is not solely coloniality's dirty work. No, it is also what emerges from a commitment to the notion that the body is an assemblage, a mass of everyone who has ever moved us, for better or for worse.

In the summer of 2015, I dated a guy, my age, who told me he loved me on the second date. I was put off, stunned; love takes time, I thought. But soon I fell in love, too. If I know anything now, it is that love is the clumsy name we give to a body spilling outside itself. It is a category we have pieced together to make something like sense or reason out of the body failing to live up to the promise of self-sovereignty.

To be "sadder than that" is thus not impossible within a scene of love-making. In the summer of 2015, I was "sadder than that," but I made love anyway and it felt like salvation. This is what indigeneity intimates: a form of love enlivened by those who are "sadder than that." This is what I wanted this book to make palpable; this is the structure of feeling I wanted to invite you into.

This Wound Is a World, then, is nothing if not a tribute to the potentiality of sadness, to showing that a body unbecome or a poetics of lateness or a choreography of mangled bodies might change the rhetoric of protest. Indeed, it echoes Jack Halberstam's provocation in his Introduction to Fred Moten and Stefano Harney's *The Undercommons: Fugitive Planning and Black Study* that "revolution will come in a form we cannot yet imagine." That is, an ethics of Indigenous resistance needs to tune into the depressed and into crying kookums and the worlds that fall from their faces. In *The Alphabet of Feeling Bad*, Cvetkovich and Karin Michalski ask: "Is it possible to share the feeling of being lonely or alone as a way to make new forms of collectivity?"[3] *This Wound Is a World* insists that it is. It insists that loneliness is endemic to the affective life of settler colonialism, but that it is also an affective commons of sorts that demonstrates that there is something about this world that isn't quite right. Loneliness in fact evinces a new world on the horizon.

NOTES

1. See http://nomorepotlucks.org/site/no-one-is-sovereign-in-love-a -conversation-between-lauren-berlant-and-michael-hardt.
2. See http://www.elle.com/culture/career-politics/a42337/angela-davis -womens-march-speech-full-transcript (emphasis mine).
3. For information on the project, see http://www.anncvetkovich.com /news/the-alphabet-of-feeling-bad.

NOTES TO THE POEMS

"Notes from a Public Washroom" draws inspiration from language in J. Jennifer Espinoza's *There Should Be Flowers*.

In "Wihtikowak Means 'Men Who Can't Survive Love,'" *i will learn to love a monster* is from "Immigrant Haibun" by Ocean Vuong.

In "Grief after Grief after Grief after Grief," point 2 is from *Lilting* (2014, director Hong Khaou). For point 7, see http://www.cbc.ca/news/canada/calgary/rcmp-gleichen-christian-duck-chief-excessive-force-1.3521620.

In "The Back Alley of the World," the final two lines use as an ideational template two lines from Bhanu Kapil's *Ban en Banlieue* (Nightboat, 2015).

In "God's River," *call it "moving"* refers to conservative pundit Jonathan Kay's suggestion that First Nations peoples should just move away from reserves as a quick fix for the social problems that saturate them.

"An Elegy for Flesh" uses phraseology from Alok Vaid-Menon's poem "When Brown Looks in the Mirror and Comes Out White."

"God Must Be an Indian" draws inspiration from language in Ocean Vuong's "Notebook Fragments."

REFERENCES

Cvetkovich, Ann. *Depression: A Public Feeling*. Durham: Duke University Press, 2011.

Halberstam, Jack. "The Wild Beyond: With and for the Undercommons." In Fred Moten and Stefano Harney, *The Undercommons: Fugitive Planning and Black Study*, 2–13. Brooklyn: Autonomedia, 2013.

Rankine, Claudia. *Citizen: An American Lyric*. Minneapolis: Graywolf Press, 2014.

Sharpe, Christina. *In the Wake: On Blackness and Being*. Durham: Duke University Press, 2016.

Simpson, Leanne. *Islands of Decolonial Love: Stories and Songs*. Winnipeg: Arbeiter Ring Press, 2014.

Stauffer, Jill. *Ethical Loneliness: The Injustice of Not Being Heard*. New York: Columbia University Press, 2016.

The Black Outdoors: Fred Moten and Saidiya Hartman at Duke University, 2016. YouTube video (2:04:02), https://www.youtube.com/watch?v=t_tUZ6dybrc. Posted by Duke Franklin Humanities Institute.

ACKNOWLEDGMENTS

Thank you to my kookum, Theresa, for flowering a world in my name.

Thank you to my mom, Roberta, some of the best parts of me are some of the best parts of you.

Thank you to my sister, Courtney, for your ability to be in two places at once.

Thank you to Micheline Maylor, my editor at Frontenac House, for, first, believing in what I had to say and, second, for allowing my artistic vision to take precedence.

Thank you to Kailen and Maura, my best friends, for standing firmly in the wildfire of me.

Thank you to Tracey Lindberg for roping me into the world of the textual. Without your steady encouragement, I might not have mustered the courage to call myself a poet.

Thank you to Jason Weidemann and everyone at the University of Minnesota Press who poured time and attention into this book: you have given it a new life.

And thank you to everyone who has picked up this book, attended a reading of mine, or googled me. Without you, books would be lonely things!

BILLY-RAY BELCOURT is a writer and academic from the Driftpile Cree Nation. He was Canada's first First Nations Rhodes Scholar in 2016 and is a PhD candidate and 2018 Pierre Elliott Trudeau Foundation Scholar in the Department of English and Film Studies at the University of Alberta. *This Wound Is a World* received the 2018 Griffin Poetry Prize and the 2018 Robert Kroetsch City of Edmonton Book Prize; it was named the Most Significant Book of Poetry in English by an Emerging Indigenous Writer at the 2018 Indigenous Voices Awards and the best Canadian poetry collection of 2017 by CBC Books. He is also the author of *NDN Coping Mechanisms: Notes from the Field*.